All City,

thank yo

I wish you countless nights

of Amazing Sex!

Author Nikki B.

# SHAKEN & SCREWED

BY

## *NIKKI B.*

This book is dedicated to my mom Lynn Shannon, my three beautiful children Nadia, SJ and Shontell. They are the reason I grind like I do. They are my biggest fans and my motivation. Also want to thank my friends for encouraging me and pushing me to stay focus and accomplish my goals.

If Sex was a Drug are you confident that you are supplying your lover with the highest dosage so that they won't go looking for a better dealer? – Nikki B.

# PRELUDE

When a man touches a woman's body there is a connection that is so intense. Yes one touch can send chills through a woman that she has never felt before. Sex is a way to fulfill and satisfy your crave for that connection. Every man shares a common weakness and that weakness being their insatiable desire for sex. A woman should always toy with this desire and find ways to feed the fire that lives inside her lover. Keep your sex life interesting and exciting!! Boring sex leads to breakups. I'm just being honest.

Sex is extremely addicting. It gives you a high and feeling you can't get from nothing else. Some require stronger dosage while other keep it basic. Find you a partner that matches your additive energy crave for sex. You can't be with a high dosage lover and make it work with a straight and narrow lover. This leads to arguments, fights and sometimes breakups. You need to have the same sex drive and open mind to keep each other entertained. Keep an open mind and be willing to try new things. Find a meeting point to keep each other satisfied. This will increase your connection and keep each other aroused.

This book will fill your head with ideas and short stories of how to please and satisfy your lover. It teaches you to have an open mind and to not be bashful or shameful in your sex life. You have nothing to be ashamed of in the bedroom. Be sexual, nasty, open, experimental, sensual, romantic, and most importantly be YOU! Find what satisfy you and your lover and make your sex chemistry amazing. Allow you erotic thoughts to lead to your everyday life. It's okay to live on the edge sexually. It's okay to be Shaken & Screwed.

In relationships if you are anything like me then you are always trying to please and satisfy your lover. So many men and women are nervous and ashamed to talk about sex when it's really a beautiful thing especially when done with someone you love and admire.

I hear woman and men not want to talk about oral sex or new positions. Some even say I am not trying this or I am not trying that. WHY NOT??? Sex is an art and there is no limit when creating a master piece.

Don't worry about how you look or your size or if what you doing you will be judged about. You should be with someone who clearly already finds you attractive and you find them attractive so let your guard down and turn up for a change.

The few ideas I discuss will walk you through how to be confident and comfortable with your lover. I will explain how to relax and just enjoy all sex has to offer. How to have fun with your lover and make memories that you will laugh about when you're older.

Once you finish reading the different steps I explain it will then be followed by a short erotic story for your pleasure to give you a visual in your mind of how to enjoy your lover. I hope you enjoy this same taste of my sexual mind.

# ORAL SEX

Let's stir some things up because let's be honest, oral sex is a MUST! I am a person that believes in catering to your partner in every sexual way and oral is best served wet. You have to know what to do and when to do it but most importantly......how to do it. So let me give you some directions downtown. Hopefully you will enjoy every minute of your sexual tryst.

**OPEN WIDE:**

Surprisingly more people than you would imagine are horrified about how they look when performing oral sex. Little do they know, whoever is receiving is not thinking about how you look they are more focused on the pleasure they are about to receive. Your partner most likely feels like you look your best because they are so turned on.

## USE YOUR TONGUE:

Men-women love the feeling of a warm tongue just as much as you do. Especially when you know what you are doing. The alphabet isn't the only thing you can spell down there. Try humming on her clit to your favorite R&B song. The vibrations will massage right into her clit and send chills all through her body. Taking her to a sexual peak that is sure to leave your face full of her sweet juices.

Women- Yes we all love a good hard dick but most men enjoy getting sucked and licked on while still soft. There is something about wrapping your lips around your man shaft allowing him to feel the warm and wetness of your mouth welcome all of him to come inside and play. It drives a man wild to actually fill EVERYTHING. Allow your mouth to wake him up. Men are very visual so be sure to stick your tongue out, spit on it, talk to him & tease him. His penis will start to rise and become hard because he will be so turned on.

## USE YOUR HANDS:

Touching the body while performing oral sex can take that moment to another level of pleasure. The aggressiveness from gripping and rubbing the thighs, ass and breast on a woman. To rubbing the chest, torso and massaging the balls on a man, will have your partners' body dancing. This allows you to show that pleasing the pussy and/or penis is the main priority but also that the body is still important.

Ladies, if you lift up his balls and lick the perineum (also known as the taint) softly, he will make noises you have never heard before. Fellas, while you are kissing on her clit slip your fingers into her vagina (maybe even a finger into her ass depending on how open your partner is sexually) I guarantee you she will not be able to stay still.

## SUCK SUCK SUCK:

From my experience getting your clit sucked on the proper way is AMAZING. When sucking on a woman's clit you should hear sounds similar to as if someone was sucking on a pacifier. The slurping and kissing effects should be passionate and wet. Remember to suck hard enough so it doesn't come out, yet soft enough so that you don't tire out your jaws. Make love with your mouth. These actions are very similar ladies when sucking a dick. When you suck, kiss, lick and pull on his penis. This rushes blood in which in return will stimulate the clit and/or penis which brings your partner closer to an orgasm. Ladies remember to deep throat your man penis allow him to fill parts of your mouth and throat that he didn't know exist. Focus, learn your body so that you can control your throat muscles. The deeper you allow him to go and the wetter your mouth becomes while sucking and pulling and teasing his dick will leave your mouth full of creamy treasure to swallow. This is how you can get a moan out of the toughest man.

**MAKE NOISE/TALK NASTY:**

You cannot, I REPEAT, you cannot be a quiet, boring oral sex giver. I can bet you a million dollars that you probably won't be giving that person oral sex anymore if you don't step outside of your boundaries to please your partner. Sex is an ART, so don't be afraid to showcase your talents. Remember don't be boring this is your main scene of your performance to turn up and show out.

Ladies if your listening to R&B music remember what I said hum to the rhythm of the beat. Deep throat his dick, adjust your throat this will allow you to swallow him whole. Spit and slurp all over his penis, the sloppier the better. Tell him how good he taste as you suck and lick up and down his dick. Allow your mouth to feed your man's EGO!! Call him daddy while giving him head. Remember sucking dick is a stress reliever and pleasure pleaser at the same time. In this moment you should become his slut. Your mouth should become his comfort zone.

Guys, we want to hear your lips smooching all around on our pussy. You know what sound I am talking about Muah Muah Muah each kiss should be moist & wet. Something like a tongue kiss except her pussy and clit is filling in for your partners' mouth & tongue. Tease her clit and talk to her as well. Tell her how juicy and sweet she taste as you finish her like a last piece of birthday cake. Your face should be covered in her icing by the last bite.

**GET MESSY:**

Ladies- Men love to see the flow of spit dripping down their dick. Some might even tell you, "Spit on it baby". Deep throating and gagging will automatically create more saliva in your mouth. As you pull his dick in and out of your mouth you will have a mouthful of saliva to keep his dick wet and messy. Kiss the bell head slowly while looking in his eyes before you wrap your lips fully around his penis and making it disappear before his eyes. This drives a man crazy some say this is the point where you snatch a man's soul. As you suck, slurp & kiss his dick allow your saliva to make a splash sound. If you want to take him to the next level throw a piece of ice in your mouth or one of my favorites is to put a hall in your mouth while giving head (yes a hall like the ones you use to sooth a sore throat) my favorite flavor is lemon. The menthol from the hall will give him an arousal like no other. Slip the hall under your tongue it will give him a cool/warm sensation while your moist mouth sucks him to his climax. Some prefer to swallow every drop something about sucking your man dry should turn you on. (At least it does for me) Now for you non-swallowers let him bust on your face or breast. Remember to always clean up your mess, every man loves a neat freak.

Men-Ladies love to see their juices all over your face. It's like we know we just served you your favorite meal. So fellas dive right into her wet vagina. This is a moment where you can't be afraid to swim, if you are baby grab a life vest so you want sink. Satisfying a woman orally is extremely important to making her reach her full climax to lead to an amazing orgasm. Women already secrete lubrication that keeps them wet so your saliva is bonus. Spread her thighs open so you can have a full view of her pretty pussy. Woman are submissive and will allow you to control her body and legs because of this repay her with full appreciation of pleasure. Kiss her pussy lips while your tongue explores the inside of her pussy until it locates her clit. Once found suck on it slowly and softly like a lollipop. Massage her thighs or grip her ass letting her know you are in full control and your focus is only on pleasing her. Hum, blow, slurp and kiss her into LaLa Land. Make her arch her back. Once her back is arched off the bed into the air you just sent her to cloud nine. "Don't let up now daddy," keep on eating her pussy continue to suck and tease on her clit until her legs start shaking. When she seems like she is running from you pull her body closer. Gripping her ass firm while your face lays deep in her pussy full of all her juices. Talk to her tell her this pussy belongs to you and she taste as sweet as a fresh cut pineapple. Just when you know she is about to cum all over your mouth awaken her inner spirit and slide a finger in her vagina while you suck her to an unknown world full of pleasure. She should be gripping the sheets, grabbing your head, screaming your name so loud that the neighbors might hear. Don't Stop!! Flick your tongue up and down catching every drip of her juices as she bust all over your face. Hopefully this has intensified your oral appetite and has you ready to eat because it's time to open wide and say AAhhhhhhhhhh……..

"Hey baby, I had a very stressful day at work so I'm home relaxing instead of going to play ball with the guys. See you soon. I love you!" was the first message on my voicemail. I felt no need to listen to the rest of my messages because I now had a mission to complete. Whenever I was having a bad day Justin would always go the extra mile to make sure I felt better. It didn't matter what it was, he just knew how to always fix it. That was something Justin and I have always been able to master, pleasing each other is what made our chemistry so powerful.

As I walked in the house, I heard the sounds of Trey Songs playing in our bedroom and the smell of my Yankee Vanilla Candle filled the air from burning on our nightstand. The steam from the shower crept from under the bedroom bathroom door and sports center was muted on the T.V. Screen. I knew I only had about 15 minutes to run into the guest bathroom and shower so I could surprise him. I washed my body in my Dove body wash, dried off and massaged coconut oil body butter from head to toe. I always keep my pussy pretty for Justin never missing a wax appointment. Looking at myself in the mirror I pulled my hair up in a high messy bun. I was on a mission. My Christina piercing at the top of my pussy always adds an extra sexy sex appeal of excitement to my naked body. Damn I have a beautiful pussy, I admired myself while putting the last touch of coconut oil on my ass cheeks. Finishing off with a few sprays of my Chanel Chance perfume. Which was of course his favorite. I closed my red silk robe tight around my waist showing my coca cola shape and nice view of my round ass that showed a little from under my robe as I walked. I like to leave my cleavage showing a little for a nice tease as well. Before leaving the bathroom I reached into the medicine cabinet and slipped three lemon halls into my robe pocket. Blew myself a kiss in the mirror before turning off the light in the bathroom. I slowly beginning dancing to the R&B music as I walked back to our bedroom. I loved the thought of pleasing my man my pussy was already throbbing and dripping wet as I whine my hips and slow danced on my tippy toes threw our door.

"Damn," I whispered to myself looking at Justin he was always fine as hell. Carmel Skin, deep waves in his hair, and muscle arms. I still get butterflies in my stomach every time I see him as if we haven't been together for almost three years. There he was laying in the middle of our bed watching football on mute while Keith Sweat was playing from our Bluetooth speaker he had it on our favorite Pandora station, all he needed was one more thing to complete his relaxation and I knew exactly what to do.

"Hi Honey" I said as I walked over to him licking my lips. He set up surprised, not knowing I was already home and ready to give him the best oral sex known to man.

"Damn Baby, I didn't know you were home already but I am so happy to see you. You look beautiful and smell amazing" he said as he leaned in to kiss me. Your man should always admire you and appreciate your efforts to look beautiful for him. Justin always complemented me. I loved that about him. "Thank You. I got your message baby, what happened today?" "Nothing serious baby, just a stubborn client of mine being indecisive about this deal we been working on for over a month. I really need to have it closed before next week baby" Justin replied with frustration all over his face.

I loosened my robe a little to allow more of boobs to become more for visible for him to see. I slowly climbed in the bed on top of him.

I began to straddle his lap, laying my moist pussy directly on top of his dick. I could feel his dick start to slowing stiffen up through his Versace boxer briefs as I continued to whine my hips to the music. I whispered in his ear, "keep talking daddy" as I slowly began to rub his shoulder and kiss on his neck. He continued, "So umm yea baby I really need this client to agree with me so we can close the deal." He begin to stutter a little not really focused on his conversation anymore but now fully focused on me. He slipped his hands under my robe and began to rub my ass. He still loved that my nipples was pierced and slowly kissed on one of nipples as I continued to massage his shoulders and kiss on his ear and neck. I lifted up onto my feet in a frog position pulling my nipple out of his mouth. I started to slowly step backwards down his body while leaning over kissing on his chest as I slowly pulled his boxer briefs down, suddenly I no longer heard him talking.

"I'm listening, keep going," I said as I positioned myself between his legs in doggy position with my beautiful yellow golden ass checks in the air. My red robe pushed up around my hips giving Justin a full view of Ass in the air. I wrapped my hands around his beautiful dick. I loved the way my pink and white French tip nails looked holding his dick. He loved it to, he kept me in the nail salon weekly. Justin really has a nail fetish my hands and feet had to always be freshly done. I looked down taking admiration of my man penis it was a caramel complexion with a perfect brown bell head. I began to kiss the tip of his dick to confirm what he already knew was about to come.

I repeated, "I'm listening baby keep going," Justin set up a little more giving his self a better view to the performance he knew I was about to put on. He said, "Oh I was done." I knew he was ready to let loose & even though we have sex daily. This was a day I wanted him to cum simply off me satisfying his orally. Making him cum off oral sex turns me on to the point that we typically climax together. I love the way he taste.

I began to kiss his bell head again as my hands massaged up and down his dick. I then stuck my tongue out giving his a wet stroke from bottom to stop, ending with sucking him into my mouth and letting my saliva drip all over his dick. Making it wet and messy how he like it. I took my left hand and massaged his balls while my right hand gripped his dick going up & down in slow circular motions with my saliva as the lubrication. The entire time I am sucking and kissing on his dick. The sounds of hearing him moan, drove me crazy. It actually made me want to give him a better performance. The fact that I knew that he loved what I was doing to him had my pussy throbbing and my juices dripping down my inner thigh. I reached down between my legs with my left hand and stuck two of my fingers inside my pussy while still sucking on his dick. I pulled my fingers out and reached up to put them in his mouth, he sucked my entire finger clean. Allowing him to taste me and confirm with him that I am enjoying this just as much as him. He looked me in the eyes and said, "Damn Girl." I could feel him moving his legs beneath me. I pulled my lips off his dick, while allowing my hands to continue to jack him off, I looked back and could see his toes beginning to curl. I let a smirk go across my face knowing he was loving every minute of this shit. If Justin knew better he knew I was just getting started.

I released his dick and slowly slid off the bed. Immediately he set up questioning me, "What you doing baby" I ignored him. Reached for the blue tooth speaker and turned the volume up a little more. I slow danced over to the dresser with my back turned to him and reached in my robe pocket and pulled out two of my halls and slid them under my tongue. Next I untied my robe and let is drop on the floor. Justin could now see the Coco Butter glistening down my spine tattoo all the way down to my nice plump ass. I slowly turned around and let him see me fully naked. My nipple, belly and pussy piercing being my only accessories. His dick was hard as a rock, calling me back to finish what I started. Justin was grabbing his dick and licking his lips.

I slowly climbed back into the bed this time from the opposite side allowing myself to still have full control of his dick and be able to look in his eyes but also have my ass and pussy in better reach and view for him to touch me while I orally pleased him.

The hall had begun to dissolve under my tongue and had my mouth now wet, warm with a cool menthol feeling. I gave him a slow deep throat followed by massive sucking up and down his dick while my hands followed my motion beneath my mouth using my saliva as double lubrication to drive him wild. He began smacking my ass and found his way to slip a finger into my vagina. I loved it and my pussy welcomed him in with a gush of wetness. I took a deep breath allowing the menthol to fully surround his dick, giving him a

warm/cool feeling of satisfaction as I deep throated him again. His

body began to squirm all over the bed. I followed by sucking slowly

but hard enough to get his blood flowing more through his dick. I

began to hum to the sounds of The Weekend's song, "What you

need" he was moaning and I was moaning because he was still

playing with my pussy, not to mention sucking his dick already

drove me crazy. My Nipples were rock hard as I pulled his dick out

my mouth to rub his dick across boobs, my nipple rings gave off a

friction that intensified his pleasure.

I told him, "Grab my hair daddy" he slowly released my bun out the

ponytail it was in flinging the ponytail holder onto the floor. I began

to go wild on his dick. He pulled my hair and lifted my chin up and

began to fuck my face. I opened my mouth wider reminding him I

was a pro. I spit and sucked faster and faster as my hands massaged

his balls and taint. I looked up at Justin and he was looking right

back at me that sent me over the edge. I kissed and sucked on his

bell head pleasing him. I lifted him balls and sucked on them too.

Making sure he was fully a mess. My big beautiful brown eyes

starred at him while his dick grew harder in my mouth and I moved faster. Splash, slurp, and suck was the noises you could hear from me sucking his dick in the most sloppy slut act possible. Women you need to be your man's nasty slut in the bedroom. ALWAYS! Spit dripped from both sides of my mouth making it super messy just how I liked it. I knew he enjoyed getting head but I think I enjoyed giving it more. Slowly jacking him off I started to fill his penis begin to pulsate, I tilted my head to the side looked him in the eyes and asked, "You ready to cum for me daddy?"

Slowly his head dropped backwards, I knew he was close. Deep throating over and over, I took his dick out again just to spit on it. I jacked off the head and started to suck on his balls while he kept saying, "Yeah baby I love that shit. You always know what to do to please daddy."

Next thing you know he set up and said, "I don't want to cum yet, lets cum together. Bring that pussy up here to my face." He turned me around and pulled my pussy to sit on his face backwards, I was in pure bliss. I loved Justin's tongue against my clit. His warm tongue caressed my clit as his hands spread my ass cheeks open giving him a full view of my lovely jewel between my legs. Justin always knew how to please me but it seems like every time he would eat my pussy it would feel new as if it was the first time. The way he kissed and sucked on my clit while sliding his finger in and out of my pussy drove me wild. He knew how to suck it rough because I was a nasty slut in the bedroom but also gentle enough to never hurt me because I was his lady. He spit in my asshole and let the saliva drip down over my pussy. As he and I continued to suck and please each other all I could hear was, "mmm hmmm mmmm hmmmm" come from him as he continued eating my pussy as if he was sucking on a piece of juicy watermelon. He pulled my waist down more to press my pussy more on top of his face as he munched away on my juices not missing a drop. I felt his arm wrap around my lower thigh and I knew what was coming next as I was still moaning, and sucking his dick. He rubbed his finger over my wet asshole where he had just spit and stuck his finger in, I screamed out, "Yes daddy!" With a mouth full of his dick my scream was muffled but he got the idea of pleasure he had just awaken inside my body. The feeling was uncanny.

"Suck that dick Angie, get that nut up out of me baby" he said as he hugged my entire lower body while he fucked me with his tongue in my pussy and finger in my ass. I could fill my climax rising inside of me. My legs began to shake and his dick beginning to pulsate. I begin sucking harder and faster knowing he would not be able to hold back any more. I adjusted my back throat muscles to suck him inside deeper so I could catch every drip drop of his cum. I pulled off and continued to jack his dick off as I lifted his balls and ran my wet tongue across his taint.

I knew his explosion was coming soon. Moaning and groaning and sucking on each other sent us into a trance. Lucky for him, Justin knew how to swim because he was about to drown and I was about to swallow. Boom, he exploded inside of my mouth. I could fill his dick pulsating and ejaculating down my throat. As my juices squirted and creamed all over his face. My legs shaking for pure pleasure did not stop my focus, which was to please him. I continued to suck and suck and suck and suck on his dick until nothing else came out. He toes was curling and he had laid his head back on the pillow and moaned, "Damn Baby." I made sure to clean him up with my tongue sucking him dry. I slipped down and went into the bedroom bathroom to grab a warm rag to clean him up. Justin was laying there looking like the King he was.

It was everything he needed and everything I wanted. I climbed back in bed with him and laid my head on his chest and asked, "Feeling Better?"

We both laughed as he grabbed me closer to him to kiss me. "Hell yea I feel better" he replied. "How about you baby?" he asked in return.

I just smiled up at him and said, "What do you think?" as I cuddled up next to him.

# ROLE PLAY

When it comes to satisfying the mind with pleasure, nothing is more exciting than the thought of role playing. The idea of bringing you or your partners' fantasy of acting like someone else brings in a new excitement that is indescribable. Role playing allows your partner to feel like he or she has more than one boyfriend or girlfriend.

It's like cheating without the bad consequences or stress that comes with it. People fail to realize that your partner most of the time steps outside of the relationship to cheat usually just for the thrill of something different. Prevent those thoughts from ever entering his and/or her mind. Learn to feed that inner fire, that thrill, that boiling desire that your lover craves.

Myself, personally I have 4 alter egos that fuel inside me sexual. My man never knows who will be coming out to be nasty.

**Nikita is the lover**, she is extremely romantic and will make you fill like a king from full body massages to catering to your every sexual desire in the bedroom. She studies everything that will make your heart, mind and dick miss her throughout the day. She will provide you with passion and pure love. (I call her The Wife)

**Nikki B. is a freak,** she is very open to learn and try out every way possible to please you she gains pleasure from the challenge of mastering how to connect with you in a sexual way no other woman has. (I call her The Pleaser)

**Kita: is your fun girl,** she is the girl that you typically can hang with all day laughing & partying. She never turns down. She will pop that pussy all day for you and keep your inner youth alive. She will dance for you in the bedroom and/or out in public. She will get drunk and fuck you in the car or suck your dick while you drive. She's always down for whatever and whenever. She doesn't like to make love because she is busy having fun and just wants to be fucked. She gone play her role as long as you treat her right. (I call her the Pretty Young Thing).

**Nicole is the slut,** she only comes out to play strictly for sexual business she allows you to take full control when making love to her. She is the most submissive of all my alter egos but also the most addicting. There really isn't much that Nicole won't allow her lover to do. She fuels off of being nothing less than nasty. If the scene isn't dirty she is not willing to arrive. (Ladies-Nicole is a special treat you give when you partner deserves her.) She shows up in the bedroom to remind my lover who the fuck I really am and remind him how much a naughty little bitch I can become. She gives off a high you cannot receive anywhere else. She is the Queen of her bedroom and will have you constantly waiting for her next dose. (I call her the Drug).

Now every woman doesn't have alter egos. These where sides of myself that I noticed as I got older. I decided to name them as I got older because the older I got the more I learned to control these alter egos and use them on my terms to please my lover. Besides my different freaky sides I love role playing. The excitement of role playing sets a spark inside you waiting to let loose. Role playing will provide a rush sure to lead to fun and pure climax from both partners. When inviting Role Playing into your bedroom you have to have an open mind. There should be no limit bringing your lovers fantasy to life.

## DECIDE THE FANTASY & SET THE SCENE:

It's totally up to you if you want to give your lover notice of the new roles you plan on playing. Either way it will be a surprise and bring a new excitement into your sex life. When giving notice, talk to your lover about how you want to be spontaneous and fulfill one of their fantasies. Once you agree upon the fantasy you are going to perform, you have to agree to perform it completely with no boundaries. There should be nothing stopping each other from creating the most sexual imaginations. Curiosity will now be on each other mind, which will lead to new level of excitement. You have to step outside of yourself and really become this new character. In order to make the fantasy be completely real you have to be willing to do it how they want, become they want it with, and deliver the fantasy where they want it at.

Now if you want to make things a little steamy, DO NOT GIVE NOTICE. You should already know what some of your lovers' fantasies are so that you can surprise him with role playing as a special treat. This is so much more thrilling because you are truly in control and hopefully your lover has an open mind and catches on to the scene and performs quickly. DO NOT BE NERVOUS, let your guards down.

## PICK YOUR NAME:

If the fantasy is of a certain image or type of person than pick a name that fits that character. If the fantasy is of a specific person........BECOME THAT PERSON.

## PICK YOUR OUTFIT AND STYLE:

When becoming this new character find something that they would wear or if the character is a specific type of image wear an outfit to bring that image in full picture. Rather its corporate casual, naughty school girl, doctor and/or nurse to prostituting slut. Doesn't matter who or what the character is as long as it gets the juices flowing.

## PICK YOUR HAIRSTYLE:

If you have short hair go grab a wig. If you hair is long switch the color up. You will be surprised on how color can add a splash of exotica.

## PICK/DECORATE THE LOCATION:

Find a location as close to the scene you are trying to bring to life. You can also decorate your bedroom to give the energy and vibe of the location. The excitement from "their fantasy" being so real will have you wanting to relocate once a week.

## GET INTO CHARACTER:

You have now renamed, redressed, restyled, and relocated yourself....you are going to have to RELAX! It's now time to put your acting skills in action and play the best role of your life in 3...2...1.

My phone had been ringing constantly for the last 5 minutes but for some reason I was in no rush to answer. There I was searching in my closet for the perfect stiletto. Anyone that knew me knew I was a shoe whore and became obsessed with having the perfect calf muscle and legs from wearing the correct pair of heels. A women in the right stiletto heel represented strength and sexiness. Any time a woman walked pass me I would instantly look down at her shoes and legs. (Okay, okay when a woman walked pass I would look at her ass as well but that's not important right now lol). Any woman that can stand in 5-6 inch heels all day was a superhero in my eyes.

"MY BABIES!!!" I screamed out as my eyes locked in on my favorite Christian Louboutin laying in the back of my closet starring right back at me. Right then I knew tonight would be a perfect night. My boyfriend Richard had been having out of town for business and I has been missing him over these few days he been gone. When he came home tonight I was gone make sure he felt special. I wanted to be different, I wanted to act different, wanted to do different things, become someone else and fulfill one of my fantasies. All of this was going through my mind as I prepared myself to, "Roleplay." This new adventure sent chills through my body of excitement yet I was

also nervous but turning back wasn't an option.

As I found the matching heel to my favorite stiletto I couldn't stop

thinking about, "Braila" his naughty school teacher who was coming

out to play. My boyfriend had always told me that fucking a teacher

was a fantasy of his, tonight I would bring his fantasy to life. My

attire was laid out across our bed. Looking in the mirror I twisted my

hair up in a knot and got all my "School Supplies" in order.

Picking up my phone I sent him a text message telling him to meet

me in the dining room, I was finishing up dinner. "Beep," I heard my

phone alert go off on my cell phone. I opened his reply message

reading, "Ok Baby, I'm in route home see you in 15 minutes."

Instantly I felt blood rushing through my body and my pussy became

wet. I looked at the clock I had about 13 minutes since the time he

sent the text message. Slipping into my red lace thong and bra

lingerie set I smiled lightly sprayed my favorite pink bottle of Bond

9 on my neck. I slipped into a tight black pencil skirt and white

buttoned down blouse. Adjusting the skirt to lay perfectly over my curvy hips, I then tied my white button down into a knot. Leaving my top three buttons undone. A peak of my pretty boobs was sitting nicely in my lace red bra. My makeup was basic yet flawless finished off with a ruby red lipstick on my lips. Opening my night stand drawer I pulled out my Gucci reading glasses and put them on my face. Standing there I looked at myself in amazement. The only thing missing was my favorite heel, quickly slipping my 6 inch stiletto on, I grabbed my papers and pen off the bed and headed down to the kitchen, Richard should be home soon.

Hearing the garage door rise, I stood there ready for action. His footsteps made my heart beat faster, I couldn't wait for his to lay his eyes on me. As soon as he turned the kitchen corner his mouth dropped. "Damn Baby" he blurted out. There I was standing in my red 6 inch stilettos, holding a stack of "graded papers" and an ink pen in my mouth.

"Welcome to class Richard! Have a seat, you're late." I said with frustration in my voice.

He stood there in shock with the sexiest grin on his face. Looking down I seen his dick print start to bulge through his pants, I smiled and continued in character. He pulled his chair out from his desk and had a seat. (The kitchen table and chair was his desk).

"You have been late to my class all week Richard" Grabbing his graded blank paper, I laid it in front of him on his desk, while saying, "Now your turning in homework incomplete."

"Richard what are we going to do about improving your grades?" I asked. Detention isn't working and you don't appreciate me tutoring you. "So I'm thinking" I began to say, "I could give you an assignment to earn extra credit so you can pass my class."

"Would you like that Richard?" I asked as I turned around and began to walk away.

As I was walking I dropped the papers on the floor in front of my desk. (Which was the island in our kitchen the left of the dining room table where he was sitting.) Quickly jumping up he rushed over to pick up the papers for me. I slid on top of the island to sit down. Crossing my legs he was able to get a peak of my lace red thong under my skirt as he stood up from grabbing the papers off the floor. He could no longer take the temptation, he tried leaning in to kiss me. I pushed him away gently with my stiletto heel on his chest. Once he seen my leg up in the air like that I just knew it was over and he wouldn't be able to hold out much longer.

Surprisingly we both continued to play our roles out. "So are you willing to do the extra credit Richard?" "We have to get these grades up." I informed him as my pen ran across his pulsating dick. Richard replied saying, "I will do whatever I have to do to bring up my grades Mrs. Braila." While trying to grab me again. He was begging through his eyes. He was loving what he was experiencing. He was READY!!!!

"You'll do what whatever I say?" I chuckled. First remember that you must turn in your best work. We're reaching for nothing less than a 100%. I leaned and whispered, "I have the perfect project for you...........are you up for the challenge?"

"Yes Mrs. Braila" he replied.

"Call me Braila" I demanded.

"Yes Braila, I can do that," "I am up for the challenge." He replied.

Untying my shirt, I opened my legs so he could see everything. My pussy was throbbing and soaking wet. You could see the moist drip over my thong. Grabbing his hand I placed it between my legs. Pulling him closing to me I whispered, "I need you to show me what Spontaneous Combustion is and if you get it right I will pass you in my class. Can you handle this assignment Richard?"

His voice sent chills through my body as he leaned in closer and replied, "I will try my hardest."

Feeling his hands began to explore all over my body was driving me wild but I had to remain in character. His lips made their way to mine kissing me with so much passion, that I could explode. With him standing between my legs I was able to reach up and pull his shirt over his head and whispered back, "Class is now in Session."

Over the rim of my Gucci glasses I looked at him as he began to lean me back across my desk. He then stated, "I want to eat lunch first."

Dropping to his knees he put his hands up my skirt to pull my thong off. "RICHARD" I moaned out loudly as his tongue did the alphabet on my clit. The humming and licking drove me crazy. He reached up to grab my ass to pull me closer to his face making his tongue go deeper inside my pussy. I was going crazy grabbing his head and ears. Richard slowly reached up pulling my breast out my bra and began playing with my nipples. Caressing my breast and nipples drove me wild and I could feel myself getting closer to my climax. Clearly so could Richard as I screamed out, "Daddy right there that's my spot baby."

He quickly stood up right as I was about to cum. I quickly set up saying, "Now that is not how you earn your extra credit Richard." Placing his hand to my lips he said, "Be patience Mrs. Braila. I just have to sharpen my pencil." As he was stating this he was dropping his pants and pulling his beautiful 9 inch dick out to assist with his assignment.

Picking me up I wrapped my legs around his waist allowing his dick to rub up against my moist pussy lips as he carried me over to his desk. Now he was driving me crazy because I wanted to fill him inside me. Standing me up, he turned me around and pushed me over his desk. Pushing my skirt back up over my waist I heard him kneel down. Rubbing both of his hands between my thighs, had me moaning and craving him. Spreading my ass cheeks open, he dived his face in eating the rest of his lunch from the back. "DAMN" I moaned out. There was that warm feeling again of me creaming all over his tongue. He knew I was about to climax.

Standing up he allowed his dick to enter my pussy like it was our first time. "Damn Braila" was all I heard as he paused to pull his dick out and enter me again. I dropped my head in disbelief as I moaned and Richard fucked me. This roleplaying has us both in outer space. Pounding my pussy he somehow still had the gentlest touch. He kiss the back of my neck while slow stroking his dick in and out of my pussy. He whispered, "What's my grade now Mrs. Braila?" I threw that pussy back onto his dick and replied, "You're

at about at 90% but as stated you need a 100% to pass my class."
Moaning and Screaming as he still fucked from the back I could feel
my legs shaking. He pushed my head down on his desk as he long
stroked me going so deep in my pussy I could feel every part of his 9
inches enter my womb. All I could yell out was, "OMG GOSH!!"

"Cum alllllll over my dick Braila. Give me that pussy" he instructed
as I did just that. Arching my back more, pushing that pussy back
and fucking him and he pounded me to pure ecstasy. I couldn't take
it anymore I wanted to lick all of my juices off of him. I tried to push
back off the table to repay the pleasure on him before we both bust.
Before I could open my mouth to ask him to let me down so I could
suck his dick. He stopped me saying, "I thought I had to do the work
Mrs. Braila, so get your ass back up there."

He cuffed by thighs pulling me to the end of the desk. Leaning over
kissing on my back he was stilling stroking my pussy, teasing my
clit gliding in and out of me. I felt his dick stiffer inside of me as I
moaned so loud. He whispered in my ear while pulling my hair and

slow stroking my pussy saying, "Did I earn my each credit yet Braila?"

I was in outer space full of pleasure and excitement from role playing out this fantasy that I couldn't respond. He flipped me over onto my back and laid me back on his desk. Sliding deep back inside my pussy. Gently wrapping his hands around my neck I felt him began to choke me softly. He knew I loved that shit. He repeated again, "What's my grades Mrs. Braila?" As he sped up and pounded my pussy causing me to squirt like never before. He still didn't stop it was a mess and all we could hear was the splash sounds of his dick sliding in and out of my vagina. My glasses was now on the floor and my legs completely in the air. I began to bite my lip and wrap my pussy muscles around his dick. Feeling my orgasm creep around inside of me ready to come out and bust on his big dick.

"I'm Cumming, I'm Cumming Richard!" I screamed out.

"Did I pass Braila?' He moaned. Now feeling his dick pulsate ready to explode.

"Yes......yes you passed now cum with me daddy" I moaned out.

I felt my pussy fill up with his warm nut as he collapsed on top of my naked body. Kissing each other passionately, we both began to laugh as we caught our breath. Richard stood up and helped me up off the desk, smacking my ass, he asked, "Baby were did that come from? What made you do this? I loved it."

Smiling I simply explained how spontaneity is a must to keep a healthy desirable relationship. On top of everything else I told him, "I wanted to do something different and exciting for you." Roleplaying is more than an act of being someone else, but it's a chance to play a new role for your lover and keep him and/or her on their toes.

# PORN & SEX TOYS

Have you ever been sitting around with your partner and they say, "Do you want to watch a Movie baby?" The next thing you know, there is a porno playing on your flat screen? Well this happens a lot and some people feel ashamed for their liking of porn. There is nothing to be ashamed or embarrassed about. Myself personally, I love Porn. To myself when feeding your mind sexually, porn is always a way to learn a ton of new ideas to try in the bedroom. Tons come with watching porn when you are in a relationship. When deciding as a couple to watch porn or use sex toys you have to be mentally ready because it's deeper than you think.

## JEALOUSY:

This is the first step to opening up the door to watching porn with your lover. You don't want your partner to think you need porn to get aroused. Let them know your interest behind watching the porn movie and why. The same goes for using sex toys. Make sure your partner is aware that the toy is there to intensify the sexual chemistry but not a requirement. The last thing you want is for your partner to feel uncomfortable or left out. When watching porn or using a sex toy make sure you show them the as much attention as you do the movie and/or toy. Doing so will make the connection deeper and an understanding will be in place.

## BE OPEN:

You are going to see some things when watching porn and/or using a sex toy that you may have never seen. CALM DOWN, it's okay because everyone is interested in different things sexually. When it comes to sex, I see that they want to label certain things weird or abnormal. In reality in the sex world normal DOES NOT EXIST. As long as you and your partner feel comfortable with what you choose to do, then you're in the clear and should have no worries.

# EXPERIMENT:

Now this part is simple. What you see is typically what you get, so try it. Everything takes some work, so if you see a position or sex toy that appeals to you then try it. You will never know how something will make you feel if you don't never do it.

Experimentation is all about seeing how things turn out. Even if its fail, at least you tried it and it will be something you and your partner sit back and laugh about. Then again it might give you a new pleasure that you never thought was imaginable and becomes something you and your lover decides to do over and over again.

# BE PICKY:

When inviting new things into your sex life or foreplay. Make sure that it is something you and your partner both enjoy. When buying a sex toy typically they are used on the female. So get something that pleases her while still exciting him by the site of her using it. My favorite being a bullet sex toy.

The vibrations on a woman's clitoris sends chills up her spine. There is something about that vibrating effect on my clit while my pussy is being sucked or fucked that has given me the best orgasms in my life. The same with picking porn make sure it is a movie that both partners will enjoy.

Rather its hard core porn, three sums, girl on girl or just a plot just as everyday reality, just make sure you both are interested so that you don't catch one of you getting bored and wanting to fast forward the scenes. Once you know what you both like, choosing porn will be easy and you're guaranteed to keep watching.

## ACT IT OUT:

Being that we all get turned on in different ways, try to glance over at your lovers face when inviting porn or a sex toy into the bedroom. Look for joy and comfortable in their eyes. Expression is always written across someone's face.

This same expression can be picked up when using a new toy or watching porn as well. You might see confusion or disgust those are signs of something you typically don't want to try again or at least not try it again without speaking to your lover and finding out what they didn't like.

Now.....when you see curiosity, excitement or even a bashful smile, take action! Those are the signs that you have just opened a new door of pleasure.

Your sex will now be more intense and exciting because you have just unlocked a new world allowing you to become your lovers' personal porn star. All things that live in the back of your mind sexually can be done.

Watching porn and using sex toys are just the tip of the iceberg but very good for beginners who are experimenting new sexual pleasures. So grab your partner, get your favorite sex toy, pop in your favorite porno and be prepared to be pleased once again just

like this…………………..

"Hey honey, what you doing?" I texted as I sat at my desk daydreaming. Waiting on his reply, I began to think of what I was going to do as soon as I clocked out from work. This evening I decided to turn it up a notch. Jason didn't have a clue of what I had on my mind. I wanted to go home, take a hot bubble bath, pop a bottle of my favorite red wine, relax and reenact some of the scenes from the porno we watched last night. Our porn collection had really grew over the last three months after we expressed our interest in watching it together.

We didn't allow it to control our relationship however we didn't mind watching it to spice up our relationship from time to time. Jason and I have a very high sex drive with an amazing sexual connection so with or without porn or passion is phenomenal. Porn just increases our sexual crave. Tonight I wanted to turn it up an additional notch as I purchased the new, "shaken & screwed lipstick bullet" on my lunch break. It was perfect being that it gave off the same effect as my other bullets with an extra tingle in vibrations but what caught my eye was how discrete it looked being that it looked like my favorite lipstick. I typically kept a sex toy bullet in my purse or car at all times. You never know when you might start missing your man and want to facetime him playing with your pussy.

I used to get bashful at times because I was scared I might say the wrong thing to turn him off. I always wondered…..Am I too nasty for him? Will he think I'm weird? And of course, he didn't think so, he actually wanted more. We discussed how in the beginning of watching porn, I would become jealous because I thought maybe he needed to watch porn first to want to have sex but that was not the case.

When I started to watch porn myself I started to understand his desire to watch it. It turned me on in so many ways. I would imagine that Jason would be doing everything the guy in the porn was doing to me. The aggression was desirable. The passion was admirable and their style of sex was just nasty how I like it. I LOVED IT!!! There really wasn't much that I wasn't keen on trying. I trusted everything about Jason he was my best friend and lover so in his arms I was open to endless sexual ideas. He loved me and loved my body, it showed every time he touched me. He took his time with me when opening new doors and I liked that. He walked me into a world I didn't want to walk out of and once he showed me I could be open with him, I never shut that door again.

"Sorry Stacy baby just now getting your message. I'm leaving the gym. How was your day? Are you still at work?" Jason replied back.

"Yes I am still at work baby. I will be leaving here in an hour. My day has been good but I am hoping you are ready to make it great!" I replied back.

I laughed as I read a number of different face expression emoji's jump across my phone screen. "I guess that's a yes baby?" I text him back.

"You know it. Clock out now baby, I will be on set waiting for you." Jason replied. I'm sure he laughed out loud just as hard as I did because we were both silly like that.

"LOL, ok director, see you soon. I Love You." I responded. "I Love you too." He replied.

Still daydreaming, I then realized I only had 20 minutes until it was time for me to clock out and leave work. I made up my mind that dinner was going to be Chinese food takeout so I didn't have to make a stop physical stop, they could deliver the Chinese food to the front door. I began packing up all my things slowly to make the time pass. I slipped my new Shaken & Screwed Lipstick Bullet into my purse.

I looked at the clock and the last 10 minutes were dragging along. Felt like an hour before 5pm would come, soon as that thought entered my mind the clocked struck 5pm. I bolted down the hallway, with a little pep in my step, my jolly ass jumped in my Range Rover, and sped off out the parking lot while the sounds of Rhianna, "Yea I said it" blasted through my speakers. I sang and danced in my seat all the way down I-75.

When I pulled into our garage the inside door that lead into the house was already open for me. I didn't have any work I needed to complete at home so I left my laptop and briefcase in the car and just grabbed my purse. I was so excited to see Jason, our love still had the new 90 day feeling even though we been together for 5 years. The sight of him still gave me those teenage butterflies in my stomach. Jason grabbed me by my arms and said, "I missed you so much today" as he placed the most seductive kiss on my lips. Before I could respond he said, "Now go do whatever you have to do to get ready. Dinner just arrived I will make our plates and put a movie in." I set my purse down on the couch and went headed upstairs to shower and change into something more relaxing.

We used to eat dinner used to eat dinner at the table every night but sometimes we would switch some things up and eat in the living room. This gave us time to sit on the couch and catch each other up on our day. When I came back downstairs there was everything set up in the living room as promised. On the coffee table was two plates, silverware, Chinese shrimp fried rice, and a nice bottle of red wine and two wine glasses. On the couch Jason was sitting waiting of me. I could tell he must have showered in the downstairs bathroom because he was in nothing but his black polo boxers, black t-shirt and black socks. I licked my lips starring at him black was my favorite color on him as he loved it on me as well. After the hot bubble bath upstairs and slipped into a short silk night gown with the matching silk robe. My body glistened from the coconut body butter and the scent of my Prada Candy perfume filled the room when I entered. Jason said, "Damn baby you smell good and look even better."

I heard what he was saying to me but my mind had started to drift off thinking about all the things I wanted to do to him. Reenacting scenes in my mind of the porno we watched last night, had me so turned on and ready to attack him. I dimmed the lights and walked over and turned the fireplace on that was attached to the television stand. I slide the porno movie and walked back to the couch to sit down next to Jason. He smacked me on the ass as I walked pass. He knew how much I loved that shit with a passion.

I really didn't have an appetite for anything other than Jason's eggroll. So I poured me a glass of wine while he made his plate and snuggled up on the couch next to him. We both began to watch as the plot unfolded. The girl on the porno was getting her cable hooked up by a cable guy while she talked on the phone to her girlfriend about her recent breakup with her boyfriend. She began to tell her friend how it has been such a long time since she had sex and that the cable guy was looking very tempting and tasty. They both laughed as if she had just told a joke but she was serious. After she ended her call she walked into the living room where the cable guy was hooking up her new DVR box and precede to flirt with him. Wearing nothing but some booty shirts and tank top with no bra and panties on underneath it wasn't long before she was in the middle of her living room floor getting her pussy ate from the back.

The moaning noises she was making turned me on so much that I had to keep squeezing my thighs together. My pussy felt like it had its own heartbeat under my robe. She had her face sideways on the carpet so we could see the expressions of pure pleasure spread across. She has the deepest arch in her back allowing her pussy and ass to be fully exposed to the cable man's face. He was licking and sucking away at her on her pussy like an ice cream cone slowly melting on a hot summer day. Hearing her moan louder as he began to play with her asshole with his thumb intensified my urge to jump on Jason. But I wanted my sexual desire to keep growing. Jason sit his empty plate back on the coffee table and pulled me in closer in his arms and started rubbing on my nipples through my robe.

The woman was moaning and screaming so loud from pleasure I knew she was about to climax. Suddenly the cable guy flipped her over onto her back, you could she her slowly try to run as he has full control. The cable guy was adamant about keeping her pussy in his mouth. He hummed and spit and licked and sucked on her pussy. Just when she was about to scream out again he pulled his dick out stuck it in her. The woman had sex toys all over her living room as she was single and clearly pleased herself in her alone time wherever and whenever in her home. The cable reached over and grabbed a butt plug and placed it in her ass while pumping away in pussy. He pussy juices were all over his dick this turned him and her own. The new pleasure of having both her holes filled at once was driving her nuts. She was shaking and screaming as he leaned in and began to suck on her perky titties. She couldn't take anymore and she couldn't wait anything for him to cum she was there she was ready. He fucked her into a sexual bliss and in return she cream and squirted all over his dick while screaming out and enjoying every minute of her orgasm.

Laughing in astonishment, she reached down pulled out the butt plug and dragged fingers back up her pussy feeling the moisture of pleasure he just helped her release. She brought her fingers to her mouth and tasted herself as the cable man smiled with a dick hard as rock starring back at her. She stood up, walked him over to her couch and whispered, "My Turn!" Dropping to her knees his dick bounced right up at attention to her plump lips. She sucked it so good, he began to stop her so he wouldn't cum to fast.

The bass in his voice made his moan send chills through her body. So she began to suck his even harder and more aggressive while her hands slowly jacked him off underneath as his dick slide in and out her mouth. The cable guy kept squirming so much that she kept stopping and asking, "Do it feel good to you baby?" He didn't say a word, he just pulled her head back with one hand and then smacked his dick all over her face with the other hand before sticking it back in her mouth.

I couldn't take it any longer. I was ready for Jason to do me the same way, if not a little rougher. During the movie I had been glancing over at Jason facial expressions the entire time. HE LOVED IT!! See oral sex always turned Jason on because he loved getting his dick sucked and he knew I loved to suck his dick. I was his nasty bitch in the bedroom and he told me it always showed. That shit drove him wild and kept our sex life exciting. It didn't matter where we were or what we were doing, if I told Jason I wanted him to pull his dick out so I could suck it, that's exactly what he did.

He must have felt my vibe because as I was beginning to undo my robe he was already standing up to pull his boxers off. His dick was just as stiff as the guys in the movie but our scene was about to be super X-Rated. My mouth began to water as I looked at his caramel dick. It was like he had giving me my own personal gold candy coated lollipop, and it was the only one in the world I craved for. Sliding down on my knees between his legs, I slowly rubbed his dick across my lips as I looked up at him. He had the sexiest grin on his face because he knew exactly what I was about to do to him.

I started to force Jason dick inside my mouth all the way to the back of my throat, so I could get my mouth as wet as possible. I let my saliva drip out the sides of my mouth, taking him deep breathes between each inch I swallowed so I could do as deep as possible. Twirling my tongue around his bell head I used my lips to keep a grip on him as I sucked and twirled. He put his arms behind his head to get a better view of my performance so I began to show off even more.

Leaning back onto my feet in a squat position I opened my mouth more, tugging at his legs he knew that this meant scout closer to the end of the couch. I began to suck his dick with no hands. Just saliva, mouth, throat and penis. Allowing his to fuck my face at an angle and my cheeks and jaws grip and pull him deeper inside my wet throat drove him wild.

I was gasping for air all while sucking and spitting all over his dick. Reaching down he grabbed my hair and shoved his deep in deeper. I choked a little from the intense force but the quick gag and adjust of my throat reflex drove him crazy, one tear dropped down my eye from the small choke but I was a pro. I relaxed and began to smack my ass and suck his dick in whirlwind. Twisting, slurping and sucking my mouth all around him drove him nuts, he moaned, "DAMN BABY!!!!"

Hearing the sounds of them fucking hardcore on the TV had me yearning to sit on his dick, so my nipple rings could glide across his chest. Not being able to wait any longer, I grabbed his dick with both hands and sucked and nice and slow all the way in my mouth and pulled it out. Kissing he bell head seductive allow my saliva to drip all over his dick and balls. I stood up so I could straddle his lap.

Jason had other plans for me. Grabbing me by the waist he lifted me into the air and laid me across the coffee table. Pushing everything to the side he kneeled between my legs and began to eat my pussy like it was the last supper. I was now watching the porno upside down of the cable man fucking the lady doggy style while Jason was licking, eating and sucking away on my clit and juices. He was licking my pussy in such slow motion with so much passion that I thought I had begun to melt like butter.

My legs began to shake so he told me to stretch them straight out allowing the heel of my foot to lay on the couch. Lying between my legs he reached back and grabbed my ankles with his hands and held my legs down. I could not move or run like the girl on TV, this was the most satisfying sexual torture. I screamed out his name so loud, "JASOOOONNNNN!!!!!" in pure ecstasy, he laughed in my pussy and kept eating.

Then releasing my ankles, Jason pushed my legs all the way in the air and told me cross them at the ankle. I did as I was told, still shaking and moaning for his sweet kisses on my clit. He spread my pussy and ass open ate all of me while sliding fingers in and out my pussy and ass hole. I could not take no more and bust all over his face and in his mouth. He just kept eating I threw my head back and moaned as I continued to climax again. I reached down pulling him up to me, gripping his jaw I licked his lips to taste my own sweet pussy juices so seductively. The look in his eyes was as if I just made him fall in love all over again. We both were enjoying every minute of it.

I put my arms around his neck and wrapped my legs around his waist. Rocking my hips and grinding my vagina against his dick I whispered in his ear, "Take your pussy baby. Make me cum all over your dick daddy." Jason dick grew even harder as he lifted me in the air laying me back down on the couch. He spread my legs completely open laying them to the sides of the couch. He has full access to nothing but pussy and ass. Grabbing my hips and sliding his dick inside of me I moaned out, "Yes daddy that's what I want!" He starts fucking me slowly each stroke I could feel his dick go deep inside me as if he was playing with my organs. I LOVED IT!! His hands holding my waist and legs fully open gave him full control he was beating my pussy up as if it stole something from him. I turned my head arching my back in pleasure and out the corner of my eye I seen my purse.

Reaching inside I pulled out my new Shaken and Screwed Lipstick Sex Toy. Jason looked at me crazy and said, "Really baby you think this is the time for lipstick?" as he leaned in to kiss me. Still sliding his dick in and out of me I almost dropped the toy because he stroke was so passionate and he was hitting all the right spots. Hands shaking I took the lipstick top off and said, "No baby I have a surprise for you. This lipstick isn't for the lips on my face." Leaning back with his dick still inside of me, he eyes grew big with excitement. I twisted the lipstick to the right and a vibration sound entered the room. Jason knew I loved bullets and this one had great reviews.

Fucking me harder and faster with more excitement by my freakiness I put the lipstick bullet directly on top of my clit. It sent chills through my body making me grip my pussy muscles tighter around his dick. This fueled his gas tank back up. He began to long stroke my pussy as I reached down rubbing the bullet all over my clit. "Jason you in my spot baby!" I screamed out. The sound was like music to our ears from the moaning, vibrating and wetness we were both ready to BUST.

I fucked Jason as if he was a brand new boyfriend. Pushing and gripping my pussy back onto his massive dick. He was so deep in my pussy that his dick disappeared. I could feel him pulsating inside of me, quickly he pulled out smacking his dick on my clit. I knew he pulled out because he didn't want to cum without me. "Spit on my pussy baby." I said. He did as I told him. Putting the lipstick inside my pussy as he spit and sucked on my clit. I was now READY and he knew it. I began rubbing on my pussy taking back full control of the bullet I whine my hips and played with my juices and his saliva while the bullet vibrated on my clit making my back arch more off the couch. "Play with the shit for daddy" he said.

The porn was still going and it seemed as like we were all doing the same things. From the sounds of the moans on the TV and the moans from me and Jason, our living room sounded like a big orgy. As he pushed his dick back inside of me once again, he began to choke me softly. The shit drove me crazy. Hurting me was the last thing Jason would so when I told him I liked being choked he was hesitant. When he seen how I reacted to being choked he became fascinated. The tone of my moan was damn near similar to a cry because everything was feeling so good. It was like he was fishing inside my body with his dick being the hook, dipping it deep inside of my pussy walls. He sucked on my neck and fucked me harder.

He dug deeper and deeper giving me stroke after stroke as I burst all over his dick. "Don't stop Jason, Don't stop baby please!!" I screamed out.

"I'm not baby. Take your dick." He said as he long stroked my pussy as I cream all over him. This turned him on. He pick back up speed, spreading my legs open more and more fucking me harder and harder.

I grabbed my sex toy again as he thrusted his dick deeper inside of me. Grabbing my hair and beating my pussy up I was ready to bust again. I laid the bullet directly on my sensitive clit and as he dug deeper. Splash, splash, Squirt I released all over his dick. I loved when I squirted, the mess we caused turned me on. Nasty was what I loved and so did Jason. "You've been a naughty girl." Jason said. "Look at this mess you created. Turn that ass over!!" He demanded.

I did exactly as I was told. My pussy still throbbing and legs still shaking from pleasure. "Toot that ass in the air so I can beat it up! And don't run baby." He instructed. The demand in his voice sent heat through my bones. I did as I was told getting in dogging positon, arching my back and putting my ass and pussy in the air.

"Yes daddy" I moaned out as Jason slide his big dick back inside of my tender pussy as he pulled my hair.

My neck was extended for him to kiss on as he held my body up and thrusted deep long strokes back inside my pussy. His dick felt bigger but I took it.......I TOOK IT ALL!!! Hearing him slap my ass as he fucked me from the back, sideways, hanging off the couch, damn near falling to the floor and he was not letting up. I loved that rough shit. From his intense pace I knew he was ready to release his sweet nut, and I had a sweet tooth.

"Tell me when you're about to cum baby, I want to taste it all." Just like in the pornos we started to talk so explicit and nasty.

"Where you want me to cum, I'm about to nut all in that pussy." Jason said in a struggling voice.

I glanced over at the television and seen the lady getting a facial shower by the cable guy. The look on the cable guy was of pure bliss. I now knew what I wanted.

"No baby, nut all over my face, I want to taste baby…..please Jason let me taste it daddy?" I plead. Carlos began to fuck me harder and faster as he yelled out, "I'M COMING!!!" I then jumped up to lay under his dick as he jack off all over my face.

My mouth was wide open catching every drop, while starring in his eyes. I licked up every drop off my lips and face that I could reach with my tongue. He had the most euphoric sense of pleasure written all over his face as he grabbed into his arms to kiss me.

We fell back onto the couch, as we heard the next scene on the porno begin to start on the TV. This one began with a guy in the shower and the guys' realtor walked in on him taking a shower. She set their playing with herself while watching him wash his body under the steamy shower. Jason and I looked at each other and at the same time and said' "Round Two." We both bust out laughing.

Our connection is amazing and we are truly each other soulmate. Everything we each wanted sexually we were open to trying and experimenting this turned both us on in ways we didn't know exist. There is no better feeling then to be able to put your guards down completely sexually, I thought for myself.

Snapping back into reality I looked up as he ran into the bathroom turning on the shower and jumping in so that my part of the movie could begin. I walked in a few moments after him butt naked shutting the bathroom door behind me.

With the shower water hitting the walls, Jason stood there dripping wet and surrounded my stream. My pussy began to throb as his dick began to stand at attention. Reaching out for me, he pulled me in and said, "Hey Realtor." I just blushed while stepping into the shower to join him and whispered, "Action!"

# About the Author

Nikki B. is an alter ego that I created, my real name is Nikita Blocker. I am an Erotic writer based out of Cincinnati, OH. Writing was always my passion started off with poetry and short stories. As I grew older erotic stories where something that I gained more interest in. I decided to write erotic because I realized how much I love sex. All parts of sex from foreplay, to oral, porn, sex toys to wild sex that will have you ready to call off work the next day LOL. Nothing was off limits in my sexual world. I am a very sexual, sensual, passionate and romantic person in the bedroom. Immediately I loved the reaction I received from sexual pleasure. There was something about the human body connecting to someone else body. Creating such a wild chemistry that turned me own in ways I didn't know existed. I wanted to Master what I loved.

I began to read erotic books and watch porn every day. I would study men and women and things that affected their relationships sexually including my own relationship. I would then use what I read or watched to master my performances in the bedroom. Pandora Box is the theme I always try to reach for when making love. Romance and being a slut in the private settings of my bedroom was the major I graduated in. I kept up on all new sexual positions that would come out and learned to have an open mind to trying new things. Sharing my freaky side with my male partners in the bedroom or talking with closest girl friends in details over a glass of wine lead to me knowing I had an inner passion I wanted to share with the world. I would hear men/women complain of being bored with their sex partner in the bedroom because every night was the same. In return I decided to answer questions and give advice on how to keep your sex drive alive and exciting.

To me sex was an Art and I wanted to be the next Pablo Picasso. Sex is one of the most powerful drugs offered to people. It can affect your attitude, happiness, stress and everyday life. To stay at the top of your game you have to provide your partner with the strongest dose of sex and best supply. This will prevent your lover from wondering off and looking for a better dealer to supply their high. I hope you enjoyed this private walk thru of my sexual mind. There will be more to come. Stay Tuned!

Made in the USA
Lexington, KY
25 September 2018